Stand Up!

Kelly Doudna

Consulting Editor, Diane Craig, M.A./Reading Specialist

ABDO Publishing Company

Published by ABDO Publishing Company, 4940 Viking Drive, Edina, Minnesota 55435.

Credits
Edited by: Pam Price
Curriculum Coordinator: Nancy Tuminelly
Cover and Interior Design and Production: Mighty Media
Photo Credits: AbleStock, Hemera, ShutterStock, Stockbyte

Library of Congress Cataloging-in-Publication Data

Doudna, Kelly, 1963-
    Stand up! / Kelly Doudna.
       p. cm. (Character counts)
    ISBN-13: 978-1-59928-742-3
    ISBN-10: 1-59928-742-0
    1. Posture--Juvenile literature. I. Title.

    RA781.5.D68 2007
    613.7'8--dc22

                                                              2006032283

SandCastle™ books are created by a professional team of educators, reading specialists, and content developers around five essential components—phonemic awareness, phonics, vocabulary, text comprehension, and fluency—to assist young readers as they develop reading skills and strategies and increase their general knowledge. All books are written, reviewed, and leveled for guided reading, early reading intervention, and Accelerated Reader® programs for use in shared, guided, and independent reading and writing activities to support a balanced approach to literacy instruction.

Let Us Know

SandCastle would like to hear your stories about reading this book. What is your favorite page? Was there something hard that you needed help with? Share the ups and downs of learning to read. We want to hear from you! To get posted on the ABDO Publishing Company Web site, send us e-mail at:

sandcastle@abdopublishing.com

SandCastle Level: Transitional

Stand Up!

Your character is a part of who you are. It is how you act when you go somewhere. It is how you get along with other people. It is even what you do when no one is looking!

You show character when you stand up straight. You have good posture as you stand in the lunch line. You sit up straight at your desk. You never slide down in your chair at the dinner table!

Lillian can balance
a book on her head.
She stands up straight.

Jada draws a picture.
She sits up straight in her
chair. Jada has good
posture.

Luis stands against the wall. He can feel that his back is straight. Luis has good posture.

Alex is reading. He sits with his back straight. Alex has good posture.

Megan keeps her
shoulders square while
she walks. That helps her
posture. Megan stands
up straight.

Stand Up!

Rachel practices
good posture
in many different ways.
She finds little
things to do
as she goes
through her day.

Rachel makes
sure she sits up
straight everywhere.
Whether at her desk
or on the floor,
she sits with care.

When Rachel
loads her backpack,
she leaves room to spare.
If she doesn't
fill it to the top,
she can keep
her shoulders square.

Rachel has
good posture.
She always
stands up straight.
She knows
it's something
that will help
her feel great!

Did You Know?

There are four different body positions. They are standing, sitting, lying face up, and lying face down.

You will have better posture if you wear both straps of your backpack. If you have to lean forward to support your backpack, it is too heavy. You should take some things out.

Even though people talk about standing up straight, there will be three natural curves in your back if your posture is proper.

Glossary

balance – to keep level without tipping to one side or the other.

posture – the position of the body.

practice – to do over and over in order to learn a skill.

square – straight and rectangular.

straight – not bent or curved.

About SandCastle™

A professional team of educators, reading specialists, and content developers created the SandCastle™ series to support young readers as they develop reading skills and strategies and increase their general knowledge. The SandCastle™ series has four levels that correspond to early literacy development in young children. The levels are provided to help teachers and parents select appropriate books for young readers.

Emerging Readers
(no flags)

Beginning Readers
(1 flag)

Transitional Readers
(2 flags)

Fluent Readers
(3 flags)

These levels are meant only as a guide. All levels are subject to change.

To see a complete list of SandCastle™ books and other nonfiction titles from ABDO Publishing Company, visit **www.abdopublishing.com** or contact us at: 4940 Viking Drive, Edina, Minnesota 55435 • 1-800-800-1312 • fax: 1-952-831-1632